# FAMOUS INVENTORS

**Newmark Learning**

629 Fifth Avenue • Pelham, NY • 10803

Printed in China.
ISBN: 978-1-60719-066-0

**For ordering information, call Toll-Free 1-877-279-8388 or visit our Web site at www.newmarklearning.com.**

## READER'S THEATER
### Multileveled Scripts

# Famous Inventors

# TABLE OF CONTENTS

**W**elcome to Newmark Learning's multileveled Reader's Theater Theme Collections. Each collection in this series offers four thematically linked Reader's Theater scripts that build fluency, comprehension, and content knowledge based on curriculum standards. Newmark Learning's Reader's Theater is unique in offering multileveled scripts that allow students at different reading levels to collaborate to build reading skills.

## The Research Behind Reader's Theater

Fluency is the ability to read a text accurately and with appropriate expression and phrasing. Fluency is important because it is directly related to comprehension. Research has shown that fluency develops gradually over considerable time and through substantial practice. Students who read and reread passages orally as they receive guidance and feedback become better readers. Studies have shown that reader's theater can effectively enhance reading fluency and, subsequently, comprehension.

## How to Implement Reader's Theater

The Reader's Theater Theme Collections make it easy to use reader's theater in your classroom. Each script comes with the following teacher's support:

- Literacy and content-area objectives
- A script summary
- A list of characters by level to help you assign the right roles to each student
- Background information to help you relate the script to content-area concepts and/or literary genres
- Staging and performance suggestions
- Literacy extensions including research, role-play, and writing activities
- Content connections
- Character education connections

## Using a 5-Day Approach to Reader's Theater

To make the most of your reader's theater experience, try a 5-day approach, providing opportunities for students to become familiar with the text and read it multiple times to build fluency and comprehension. A suggested pacing plan is provided on the next page.

# Five-Day Lesson Plan for Using Reader's Theater

| Day | Focus | What to Do |
|---|---|---|
| **1** | **Introduce the Script** | • Give each student a copy of the script.<br>• Have students skim through the text looking at the organization and the illustrations.<br>• Share the background information provided, as needed, to prepare students to read. |
| | **Introduce Vocabulary** | • Read the words and definition in the glossary for the script, and ask students to use the words in sentences. |
| | **Model Fluent Reading** | • Ask students to listen and follow along with you as you read the script aloud to model fluency and expression. |
| **2** | **Build Fluency: Echo-Read** | • Read the script aloud, and ask students to echo-read, or repeat, the lines after you. Stop when necessary to explain vocabulary.<br>• Call attention to the different types of punctuation marks and model how to read them. |
| | **Build Comprehension** | • Ensure students understand the ideas in the story, as well as character development, by involving them in a discussion. For example:<br>*How would you describe the characters?*<br>*What was the play mostly about?*<br>*How did the characters change?*<br>*What happened when . . .* |
| | **Build Vocabulary** | • Make sure students fully understand the glossary terms. |
| | **Assign Roles** | • Use the reading levels provided for each script to help you assign roles that support or challenge each student appropriately. |
| **3** | **Choral-read for Fluency** | • Involve students in a choral-reading of the script to reinforce fluency. Remind students to use dramatic expression to bring each character's mood or personality to life. |
| | **Rehearse the Script** | • Use small-group time for students to rehearse their script. Monitor students as they rehearse, and offer suggestions for expression, voice, and characterization. |
| **4** | **Rehearse the Script** | • Use small-group time for student rehearsal. Do not interrupt this second rehearsal, but simply observe students as they read.<br>• Use the assessment rubric on page 91 to monitor students' rehearsal behavior and reading fluency. |
| | **Staging and Performance** | • Decide on a stage area, how students will be positioned, and whether props or movements will be added. See Staging and Performance Suggestions provided for each script. |
| **5** | **Perform the Script** | • Invite students to present the script to an audience of other class members, students from other classes, school staff members, and/or parents.<br>• Use the assessment rubric on page 91 to monitor students' rehearsal behavior and reading fluency. |

# Assessing Student Progress

The Reader's Theater Assessment Rubric on pages 91-92 helps you evaluate student progress in all areas of fluency. Included on the rubric is a rating scale for assessing:

- **Phrasing and Fluency**
- **Intonation**
- **Listening**
- **Pace**
- **Accuracy**
- **Characterization**
- **Behavior**

# Literacy, Content, and Character Education Connections

Each script has script-specific literacy and content extension activities based on the script. Select the activities that will benefit your students the most.

Each script also has a character education connection. Some of the core concepts and ethical values addressed within the scripts are listed here:

- **Trustworthiness:** integrity, honesty, reliability, loyalty

- **Respect:** follows the Golden Rule, tolerance, acceptance, nonviolence, courtesy

- **Responsibility:** accountability, perseverance, self-control, does the right thing

- **Fairness:** open-minded, just, shares, plays by the rules

- **Caring:** kind, considerate, compassionate, helpful, charitable, expressed gratitude

- **Citizenship:** involved in school and community affairs, volunteers, cooperates, respects authority, protects the environment

# Ben Franklin's Visit

## Summary

As this time-travel story opens, Mrs. Peters's class is studying Benjamin Franklin. Lewis's time machine, called the *When Machine*, goes back in time to bring Ben Franklin to the present, along with John Adams, Abigail Adams, Thomas Jefferson, and Sally Franklin, Ben Franklin's daughter. As a result of the visit, the students learn about many of Franklin's accomplishments and contributions, such as helping to write the Declaration of Independence and the Constitution; experimenting with electricity; and inventing the stove, bifocals, and the lightning rod. And Franklin himself gets a hands-on experience with modern technology!

# Ben Franklin's Visit

## Objectives

### Literacy

Students will:

- Develop fluency and expression
- Understand characters' motives, actions, and feelings
- Relate their reading experience to what they already know about Benjamin Franklin

### Science

Students will:

- Learn about Benjamin Franklin and his many contributions

### Character Education

Students will learn about:

- **Citizenship**—work to make your community better
- **Gratitude**—thank others for their help

| Characters | Reading Levels |
| --- | --- |
| Lewis | F |
| Jenny | G |
| Alison | G |
| Tommy | H |
| Carlos | H |
| Ben Franklin | I |
| Tammy | I |
| Abigail Adams | J |
| Sally Franklin | J |
| John Adams | K |
| Thomas Jefferson | L |
| Mrs. Peters | M |

# Background Information
## Benjamin Franklin

Franklin was a writer, statesman, scientist, inventor, printer, and post-master. He was one of our country's founding fathers and one of our greatest citizens. Franklin was born in 1706 in Boston but lived most of his life in Philadelphia. He died in 1790.

Franklin remained a printer nearly all his life and took great pride in his profession. In 1730 he published the *Pennsylvania Gazette*, which became one of the major newspapers in the Colonies.

Franklin is known for his work with electricity, although he was nearly killed by his early experiments with lightning. His single fluid theory led to the electron theory of 1900. He had to invent terminology to go along with his experiments in electricity. The terms included battery, charged, condense, conductor, positively, and negatively.

In addition to his work with electricity, Franklin invented many other items that are part of our lives today. His inventions include the Franklin stove, first called the Pennsylvania Fireplace; a writing chair with an arm on one side for writing; an odometer; a library stepstool; bifocals; and a mechanical arm for reaching books on high shelves. Franklin could play the violin, harp, and guitar, and he invented the glass harmonica, which is played by touching the edge of a spinning glass with a wet finger.

Franklin was dedicated to public service. He started the first volunteer fire department, the first public library, and the first insurance company in America. He raised money to start the first hospital in America, and he founded the University of Pennsylvania. He improved the postal service and was deputy postmaster for the Colonies between 1753 and 1774. He was president of the Abolitionist Society and worked to abolish slavery.

Franklin was a statesman, and he was the chief delegate to the Albany Congress of 1754, the first conference to discuss a confederacy of colonies. He was one of the delegates to sign the Declaration of Independence. During the Revolutionary War, he served as minister to France, where he was able to get monetary support from France for the war. He served in the Pennsylvania Assembly until his death.

# Staging and Performance Suggestions

- Have students who are reading the parts of the students and the teacher stand together in a group facing the audience. The characters in the past can stand to the side of them with their backs to the audience. When it is time for them to appear, they can turn and face the audience.

- Costumes could be used to differentiate the people in the present from those in the past. The students and teacher could wear ordinary clothes. The women from the past could wear long dresses, and the men could wear long coats.

- Students could add sound effects to signal the arrival of the time machine.

# Literacy Extensions

## Role-play an Interview

Have students suggest a famous person from the past that they would like to interview. Have students work in pairs to write questions they would like to ask. Students could then research the answers to the questions and present a role-play where one student acts as the interviewer and the other student acts as the famous person and answers the questions.

## Write a Letter

Have students think about what they would say to Ben Franklin if they met him in person. Have them put their thoughts into a letter written to him.

# Content Connections

## Science

History tells us that Franklin was tired of changing glasses to look far away and then up close. He cut the lenses from a pair of "distance" glasses in half, and did the same with a pair of "up-close" glasses. He then glued the top part of the distance lens to the bottom part of the up-close lens. Now he could look far away and up close without having to change glasses.

## Character Education Connection

- Ben Franklin had many ideas that made life better in his community. Who makes things better for people you know? Write a letter to that person, thanking him or her for making your community better.

- Ben Franklin was a good citizen because he made his community better. What do you do to be a good citizen in your school or community? Think of one thing you can do today to be a good citizen

- Ben Franklin says, "Thank you all for recognizing my place in history!" He says thank you to show gratitude. What do you do to show gratitude?

# Ben Franklin's Visit

## CHARACTERS

| Ben Franklin's Time | Today |
| --- | --- |
| Abigail Adams | Mrs. Peters |
| John Adams | Alison |
| Sally Franklin | Carlos |
| Thomas Jefferson | Tommy |
| Ben Franklin | Tammy |
| | Lewis |
| | Jenny |

## SETTING

a social studies class

**Mrs. Peters**: Class, today we're going to talk about Benjamin Franklin. Then you'll be ready to write your reports.

**Alison**: Writing reports is so boring.

**Carlos**: Wouldn't it be cool if we could really meet Ben Franklin?

**Tommy**: We can! Tammy and I have an idea we think will be fun.

**Tammy**: Our friend Lewis invented a machine that can go back to the past and ahead to the future.

**Tommy**: We call it the *When Machine*.

**Tammy**: Right now Lewis is on his way back from 1787 with some of Ben Franklin's closest friends. Then he'll go back for Ben Franklin.

**Mrs. Peters**: We'll be able to get a firsthand account of the life and times of Ben Franklin.

**Tommy**: Here's Lewis now!

**Lewis**: Hi, everybody! Come and meet our guests!

**Mrs. Peters**: It's John and Abigail Adams!

**Lewis**: And Thomas Jefferson, too!

**Alison**: John Adams was the second president of the United States.

**Tammy**: And Thomas Jefferson was the third president.

**Students**: Hi, Mr. Adams! Mrs. Adams! Mr. Jefferson!

**Mrs. Peters**: And this must be Sally Franklin, Ben's daughter.

**Abigail**: My goodness! How strange everything looks!

**John**: It is remarkable. But Lewis, you are going to bring us home, aren't you?

**Lewis**: Of course!

**Jenny**: Are you really from the past?

**Carlos**: You're not special effects or anything, are you?

**Sally**: Is my father here yet?

**Tommy**: Not yet. Lewis is going back to get him right now.

**Abigail**: I think it's wonderful that you young people are writing and learning about Ben Franklin.

**Tammy**: We want to ask him lots of questions and show him how much people think of him today.

**Jenny**: Could you please tell us some things Ben Franklin did in your day?

**Jefferson**: He fought for independence his whole life.

**Abigail**: He helped write the Declaration of Independence in 1776.

**John**: After the war with England, he helped make peace with other countries.

**Jefferson**: He also helped write the United States Constitution.

**Alison**: That's a lot right there!

**Sally**: But Father always said his most important job was helping people.

**John**: Who can tell us something else Ben Franklin did?

**Jenny**: He invented bifocals in 1784.

**Carlos**: Bifocals are glasses that let people see close and far away at the same time. They are popular today.

**Alison**: He invented a stove in 1744. We even call it the Franklin stove.

**Carlos**: It gives more heat than a fireplace, and it uses less wood.

**Abigail**: We have one at our farm.

**Jenny**: And we have one in our family room.

**Sally**: I remember the time Father flew his kite in a storm.

**Tammy**: He wanted to find out what lightning was.

**Carlos**: He proved that lightning is electricity!

**Jenny**: Electricity is what lights our homes and makes our TVs run.

**John**: TVs? What are TVs?

**Abigail**: Relax, John. Remember, this is the future.

**Sally**: Don't forget that my dad's famous experiments led to his invention of the lightning rod.

**Tommy**: Ben Franklin also helped people learn. I got these books from the library.

**Jefferson**: Do you all have libraries in your homes?

**Carlos**: No. We no longer have to.

**Tammy**: Thanks to Ben Franklin, we have public libraries. He created the first public library in America.

**Alison**: He also founded the University of Pennsylvania in Philadelphia.

**Jenny**: He helped sick people, too.

**Sally**: He started the first free hospital in America in 1755.

**Carlos**: It's still open today.

**Mrs. Peters**: He was also one of the first postmasters in America.

**Alison**: Before then, people got letters only two times a year.

**Jefferson**: Because of Ben, people got letters every week.

**Alison**: We get mail nearly every day.

**Mrs. Peters**: Ben Franklin was also a writer. Who remembers some of his famous sayings?

**Tommy**: I know one. "Little strokes fell great oaks." That means you can get a big job done with lots of small steps.

**Alison**: He also wrote, "A penny saved is a penny earned."

**Carlos**: Save money today, so you'll have some tomorrow.

**Tammy**: Here comes Lewis with Ben Franklin!

**Lewis**: Everyone, let's welcome Ben Franklin!

**All**: Welcome, Ben Franklin!

**Ben**: Wow! Look who's here! But tell me, where am I? Lewis wouldn't say.

**Abigail**: You're in the future, Ben. We've been talking about all the important things you have done.

**Ben**: I am very honored.

**John**: You're almost 300 years old now, Ben.

**Ben**: I look pretty good for 300, don't you think?

**Sally**: People remember you, Father, even after all these years.

**Lewis**: We sure do! And we bought you a present.

**Ben**: How wonderful! I love presents!

**Lewis**: We know you like to write. So we got you a laptop computer.

**Ben**: A what?

**Carlos**: A computer! You can use it to type words. It's faster than pen and ink.

**Jenny**: It runs on electricity.

**Ben**: Ah, yes, electricity! I knew the results of my experiments would be put to good use.

**Alison**: You can use the computer to send e-mail to anyone you want.

**Tommy**: And you don't need stamps!

**Jefferson**: I wish we could have sent an e-mail to King George of England.

**Abigail**: We would have told him a thing or two!

**Ben**: I'm going to write an e-mail this very minute.

**Sally**: Who are you going to write to, Father?

**Ben**: To all of you.

**Jefferson**: What will your e-mail say?

**Ben**: It will say, "Thank you all for recognizing my place in history!"

**Mrs. Peters**: Thank you, Ben Franklin, for your contributions to society—as a writer, an inventor, a scientist, a patriot, and a statesman!

**The End**

READER'S THEATER
**Multileveled Scripts**

# GLOSSARY

**bifocals** (BYE-foh-kuhlz): eyeglasses with lenses that have two sections, for seeing up close and farther away

**electricity** (e-lek-TRIS-uh-tee): a form of energy used for heating and lighting, and for making machines work

**experiments** (ek-SPER-uh-ments): scientific tests used to try a theory or see the effect of something

**hospital** (HOSS-pi-tuhl): a place where people receive medical treatment and are looked after when sick or injured

**lightning** (LYTE-ning): a flash of light in the sky caused when electricity moves between clouds or between a cloud and the ground

**postmaster** (POHST-mass-tur): the head of a post office

# Thomas Edison Invents the Lightbulb

## Summary

The play begins in the fall of 1879. Newspaper reporters question Edison about his promise to invent a long-lasting electric lightbulb by New Year's Day 1880. For the next few months, young Edison and his assistants work day and night. They test thousands of substances, but everything they try breaks the bulb or burns up quickly. Although his assistants grow discouraged, Edison calmly goes on. Just before the deadline, Edison discovers that carbon-coated cotton thread will work. The world is thrilled by the electric light. It is another brilliant success for the "Wizard of Menlo Park" who went on to invent many other machines that are an important part of modern life.

# Thomas Edison Invents the Lightbulb

## Objectives

### Literacy

**Students will:**

- Develop fluency and expression by practicing text at an appropriate reading level
- Understand characters' motives, actions, and feelings

### Science

**Students will:**

- Be introduced to some basics of electricity, such as conductors
- Recognize that inventing takes hard work and long hours
- Understand how inventions can benefit society

### Character Education

**Students will learn about:**

- **Perseverance**—keep trying and never give up, though the task seems too difficult
- **Reliability**—do what you say you will do

| Characters | Reading Levels |
| --- | --- |
| Newspaper Reporter 1 | I |
| John | J |
| Newspaper Reporter 2 | J |
| Thomas Edison | K |
| Charles | L |
| Narrator | L |

# Background Information

## Thomas Edison

### Edison and Light

Although Thomas Edison did not invent the lightbulb, he created the first practical, long-lasting lightbulb. Edison's lightbulb was reliable and cheap and could be used in the home. Earlier bulbs did not burn long or were too powerful for home use.

What is more remarkable, Edison, ever the practical inventor, developed all the elements needed to bring electric light to the public. He improved the generator, a machine that changes mechanical energy into electrical energy. He made the parallel circuit, which carries electric current. Edison also created light sockets with on-off switches and safety fuses. Without these inventions and others, electricity could not have lit the world.

### Edison's Gifts to the World

Edison was curious about everything, especially science. He had a questioning mind and wanted to know how things worked. The hard-working young man was also very practical. He knew that his inventions had to be useful or they would not sell.

After his early successes with inventions that improved the telegraph, Edison established his "invention factory." He brought together in one place everything and everyone he needed for inventing. His complex had scientists, labs, machine shops, an office, and a library. Edison and his team began turning out many inventions. The invention factory was itself a brilliant invention and the world's first industrial research and development center.

Edison holds many records. He received the most U.S. patents for inventions (1,093). He is the only American to have a patent granted every year for 65 straight years (1868 to 1933). It is no surprise that *Life* magazine declared him "Number One Man of the Millennium."

# Staging and Performance Suggestions

- Use a table for Edison's lab. Actors can stand in front of it for press conferences and behind it for lab work.
- Have the Narrator stand at stage left. Use center stage for the action.
- For a backdrop, use a white sheet with black marker drawings of lab equipment such as burners and test tubes.
- Have the Reporters use pencils and small notebooks as props.

# Literacy Extensions

## Words of Wisdom

Thomas Edison is remembered for wise sayings such as these:
   "Genius is 1% inspiration and 99% perspiration."
   "I can never pick up a thing without wishing to improve it."
   "There's a better way to do it. Find it."
Have students work with a partner. Ask each pair to choose one of these sayings and explain what it means.

## The Greatest Inventions

What do you think is the greatest invention? The computer, the telephone, the car? On a sheet of paper, draw a picture of the invention and write its name, what it does, and why you think it is so important. Post your paper with your classmates' on a bulletin board titled Great Inventions.

# Content Connections

## Physical Science

Light is energy released by an atom. Tiny packets of light, called photons, are like particles, but they have no mass. Atoms release photons of light when one or more of their electrons become excited. Electrons are moving atom parts with a negative charge. Electrons can be made to flow in a wire to produce electric current.

Electric current flows into the base of a light bulb and is passed on through stiff wires. The wires are attached to a very thin, long filament, or strand of wire. The filament is coiled up to fit inside the bulb, and it is held up by a glass mount, or rod. The filament is made of tungsten, a metal that will become very hot but will not burn up. Electrons zip through the filament and bump into tungsten electrons. As they heat up, the electrons release energy in the form of heat and light.

# Character Education Connection

• Edison and his inventions helped make the world a better and safer place. Tell about an idea you have to make your school or community better. Describe what you can do to make your idea happen.

• Edison never gives up on his plan to make a better lightbulb despite thousands of attempts that don't work. Why do you think he kept on trying, in spite of all the disappointments?

• Edison also does what he said he would do: he makes an improved lightbulb by his New Year's Day deadline. Why is doing what you say you will do important? What will it make people think about you?

# Thomas Edison
## Invents the Lightbulb

### CHARACTERS

Newspaper Reporter 1

Thomas Edison

Newspaper Reporter 2

Narrator

Charles

John

### SETTING

Menlo Park, New Jersey, 1879–1931

**Reporter 1:** Mr. Edison, do you mean that?

**Edison:** Without a doubt.

**Reporter 2:** You will light up your lab by New Year's Eve, 1879?

**Edison:** It will be as bright as day.

**Reporter 1:** With glass bulbs, using electricity?

**Edison:** Indeed!

**Reporter 2:** That is some promise. New Year's Eve is only a few months away.

**Reporter 1:** What's wrong with gas lamps? They light our homes. Our streets. Our offices.

**Edison:** They cost too much. They are dirty.

**Reporter 1:** How so?

**Edison:** The gas in lamps makes soot. It gets all over the house. On the furniture. On the floors. On the walls.

**Reporter 2:** Gas is the best method we have.

**Edison:** I can do better! Gas lamps cause fires. People get hurt. It's time for a change.

**Reporter 1:** You seem so sure that you can perfect the electric light.

**Reporter 2:** You're not the first inventor to make a lightbulb.

**Edison:** Those lightbulbs burned out too fast. I will make a bulb that will last a long time. I believe my assistants and I can do it. I know we can do it. Come back to my lab on New Year's Eve.

**Reporter 1:** We'll be there.

**Narrator:** Back in 1879, many people thought Edison would fail. But he had proved he was smart. He invented the phonograph in 1877. It was an amazing invention for its time. People gave Edison a nickname.

**Reporter 1:** You are the Wizard of Menlo Park.

**Narrator:** Menlo Park is in New Jersey. It is where Edison set up his lab.

**Reporter 2:** After all, you are a genius.

**Edison:** A genius? What's a genius?

**Reporter 2:** It's a gifted person.

**Edison:** Nonsense! Being a genius means nothing more than working hard. I say it is one percent inspiration and 99 percent perspiration.

**Reporter 1:** Perspiration?

**Edison:** Yes, the sweat from working hard. Now, I have work to do.

**Narrator:** Edison and his assistants keep working. They work hard. Edison is rich, but he still loves to invent. Sometimes, he works all night. Weeks pass.

**Charles:** Thomas, you told the reporters we would create an electric lightbulb that doesn't burn up quickly.

**John:** But that means we must find the right conductor to put inside the bulb.

**Charles:** Yes, that's a material that lets electricity pass through it.

**John:** The conductor must heat up and give light.

**Charles:** But not burn up and break the bulb.

**Edison:** I am not worried.

**John:** But we are! If we don't find the right conductor, the bulbs will keep . . .

**Narrator:** Suddenly, there is a loud sound in Edison's lab! Pop . . . pop, pop, pop!

**John:** . . . bursting.

**Narrator:** Again, the lightbulbs break. Edison and his assistants keep trying.

**Charles:** We have tried thousands of different things to light inside the bulb.

**John:** Straw. Bits of wood. Even hair from a man's beard.

**Charles:** Time is running out! People will laugh at us on December 31!

**Edison:** We will try something else. Keep going. I know we will find the answer.

**John:** We even used fishing line.

**Charles:** And last week, we tried plants from across the sea.

**John:** Thomas, you work twenty hours a day. But we still do not have a lightbulb that people can use.

**Charles:** What will happen when the reporters come on December 31? It won't be a happy new year.

**John:** They will say we have failed.

**Edison:** We have not failed. We have found ten thousand ways that won't work.

**Narrator:** A few weeks later, Edison is still in his lab, working. Finally, he has a breakthrough.

**Edison:** We need to find a conductor for our bulb. It must glow with light but not burn up.

**Charles:** Right.

**Edison:** So, let's coat this cotton thread with carbon. Why do you think we should try that?

**Charles:** Because carbon will glow for a long time without burning up.

**Edison:** Correct. Now, what does everything need in order to burn?

**Charles:** Oxygen, of course. From the air.

**Edison:** So when we take out the air from this bulb—

**Charles:** The thread should glow. But not burn.

**John:** Brilliant, Mr. Edison! But will it work?

**Edison:** There's only one way to find out.

**Narrator:** Edison pulls a switch. The thread coated with carbon heats slowly. It begins to glow. Brighter and brighter.

**John:** It's not going out!

**Charles:** And the bulb isn't breaking.

**John:** Mr. Edison, you are a genius!

**Narrator:** That bulb stays lit for forty hours. Finally, December 31, 1879, arrives. Reporters and others gather at Edison's lab. They want to see Edison's latest invention. Will he do what he promised them months ago?

**Edison:** Everyone. Watch this!

**Narrator:** With the flick of a switch, two thousand bulbs light the building. The crowd gasps.

**Reporter 1:** It is nighttime outside but as bright as day in your lab! I must write my story now.

**Reporter 2:** My headline will read: "The Great Inventor's Triumph."

**Reporter 1:** And mine: "Thanks to Edison, a Bright New Day Has Arrived!"

**Reporter 2:** Thomas Edison, the Wizard of Menlo Park, has changed the world. And he is only thirty-two years old.

**Reporter 1:** Edison keeps inventing for many years. He gets very rich. His fame grows.

**Reporter 2:** In time, electric lightbulbs spread across America and to other countries. Electric lights become safe and cheap. Gas lamps are a thing of the past.

**Narrator:** And when Edison dies in 1931, the world mourns. To honor him, President Herbert Hoover has the lights in New York dimmed. This is to pay respect to a special man. Today, Edison's lab in Menlo Park is a museum.

**Reporter 1:** Edison invented more than one thousand things: An electric generator.

**Reporter 2:** The first motion pictures. A talking doll.

**Narrator:** But mostly, people recall that Edison brought electric lights to their homes. And stores. And streets. The genius in his lab in Menlo Park brought electric lightbulbs to the world.

## The End

**READER'S THEATER**
**Multileveled Scripts**

# GLOSSARY

**conductor** (kun-DUCT-or): a material that lets electricity go through it easily

**dimmed** (DIMD): made dark

**electricity** (i-lek-TRISS-uh-tee): energy that comes from a flow of an electric charge through a conductor

**genius** (JEEN-yuhss): a gifted person

**inspiration** (in-spuhr-AY-shun): something that brings about thought or action

**invention** (in-VENT-shun): something new that didn't exist before

**phonograph** (FOH-nuh-graf): an instrument that reproduces sound recorded on a grooved disk

**soot** (SUT): a black material that comes from things that burn

# The Wright Brothers at Kitty Hawk

## Summary

Tammy and Tommy are about to go on a time-travel adventure. They plan to take the When Machine back to Kitty Hawk, North Carolina, to the year 1903. They want to learn more about the Wright brothers and their historic flight. Their friend Lewis, who invented the *When Machine*, doesn't want to go along, but he gets caught in the machine and ends up accompanying his two friends. When the trio arrive at Kitty Hawk, they find Orville and Wilbur Wright struggling to free the rudder of their plane from the sand. They help the brothers free the plane. Orville and Wilbur describe how their plane works, and Tammy and Tommy tell them about the wonders of flying in the future. After the trip, Lewis decides he wants to be a regular traveler in the When Machine.

# The Wright Brothers at Kitty Hawk

## Objectives

### Literacy

**Students will:**

- Develop fluency and expression
- Understand characters' motives, actions, and feelings
- Relate what they know about the Wright brothers to their reading

### Social Studies

**Students will:**

- Learn about the Wright brothers
- Learn about flight

### Character Education

**Students will learn about:**

- **Citizenship**—do your part to make the world better
- **Critical thinking**—make decisions based on reason

| Characters | Reading Levels |
| --- | --- |
| Tommy Time | I |
| Tammy Time | J |
| Wilbur Wright | J |
| Orville Wright | K |
| Lewis | K |

# Background Information

## The Wright Brothers

Wilbur Wright was born in 1867 and Orville in 1871. When their mother became sick, Wilbur put off college to care for her. Orville dropped out of high school to open his own print shop in 1889. In 1890, Wilbur joined the business as an editor, and the two published a local newspaper.

In 1894, to augment their printing business, they started a business repairing and selling bicycles. This soon became a successful business and they began manufacturing their own bikes.

The huge interest in flying machines captured the attention of the Wright brothers. All the aircraft that had been flown at that time were ones that lacked controls. Wilbur devised a system that allowed the plane to roll to the right or left. They tested this first with a kite and then in a series of gliders.

The tests with the gliders were disappointing because the gliders were unable to get enough lift. The Wright brothers developed a wind tunnel in which they could do experiments to determine the correct wing shape and get the right amount of lift. On December 17, 1903, the brothers made the first sustained, controlled flight in a powered aircraft.

Over the next years, the brothers continued to perfect their plane. In 1905, they flew the first practical airplane. They tried to get a contract with the U.S. government but were turned down. In 1907, they finally got a contract to build an aircraft for the U.S. Army. The Wright brothers made many public flights that put them in the news, although these years were stressful and included fights over patents. In 1912, Wilbur died from typhoid. Orville sold the Wright Company in 1916 and went back to inventing. He died in 1948.

# Staging and Performance Suggestions

- Find appropriate music, such as "Those Magnificent Men in Their Flying Machines," to play as a lead-in to the reading of the play. Fade the music out before the first reader begins to read. The music could be faded back in at the end of the play.

- The characters of Orville and Wilbur could be frozen on one side of the stage. They might kneel to illustrate work being done on the rudder. The characters of Lewis, Tammy, and Tommy could walk over to them after reading the last lines on page 57, as Orville and Wilbur become animated and read their lines.

# Literacy Extensions

## Read about Icarus

One of the earliest stories of human flight is that told by the ancient Greeks. It is the story of Icarus. Have students read the story and discuss the lesson that it teaches.

## Write a Newspaper Account

The Wright brothers didn't tell the press about their flight because they wanted their hometown newspaper, the *Dayton Daily News*, to run the story. But the paper refused to report it. Word got out about the flight anyway, and several newspapers printed inaccurate stories. The *Dayton Daily News* ran the true story the following day.

Have students write an article that could have appeared in the newspaper on December 18, 1903. Make sure they have all the facts for their article. Encourage them to write a catchy headline and identify who, what, where, and when in the first paragraph.

# Content Connections

## Science

The principle that forms the basis of all flight is called Bernoulli's principle. Daniel Bernoulli was a Swiss scientist who lived in the 18th century. According to this principle, the pressure in a moving stream of fluid (air) is less than the pressure in the surrounding fluid (air). An airplane's wing is designed so that the air passing over the wing travels faster than the air passing beneath it. Thus the pressure below the wing is greater than the pressure above the wing and an upward force is created.

# Character Education Connection

- Orville and Wilbur tried to fly many times before they succeeded. They showed perseverance when they kept on trying. Write about a time you kept working at something that was hard for you. Why did you persevere? Would it have been easier to quit? Why or why not?

- Orville and Wilbur Wright changed the way we travel. Think of someone else who has made the world better. Tell the class about how that person made a difference.

- The Wright brothers built the first airplane using critical thinking, or making decisions based on reason. Why is it important to use critical thinking?

# The Wright Brothers
## at Kitty Hawk

**CHARACTERS**

Lewis

Tammy

Tommy

Orville Wright

Wilbur Wright

**SETTING**

The present and Kitty Hawk, North Carolina, in 1903

**Lewis**: Tammy! Tommy! Get up!

**Tammy**: Lewis, it's Sunday. We don't have to go to school.

**Lewis**: You haven't done your report on the Wright brothers yet.

**Tommy**: Oh, no! It's due tomorrow. Maybe Mom and Dad can help us.

**Lewis**: They're still back in 1776. They took their *When Machine* to see Ben Franklin, remember?

**Tammy**: What are we going to do?

**Lewis**: Take your own *When Machine*. Learn for yourselves.

**Tammy**: Good idea. We can go see the Wright brothers' first airplane flight.

**Tommy**: Is the *When Machine* ready?

**Lewis**: I had an idea you'd be going. It's set for December 17, 1903, Kitty Hawk, North Carolina.

**Tammy**: Lewis, come with us this time. The *When Machine* is safe.

**Lewis**: I know that! I built it. But I don't do time travel.

**Tammy**: OK. We'll see you when we get back.

**Lewis**: Ready? Here you go! Oh, no! I forgot to release the brake!

**Tammy**: Lewis! You came after all.

**Lewis**: I didn't mean to. I had my hand on the brake when WHOOSH!

**Tommy**: Well, since you're here, could you help us with our report?

**Tammy**: Who were the Wright brothers? Our book says they sold bicycles.

**Lewis**: They didn't just sell bicycles. They designed and built them, too. And they've been building gliders for years.

**Tommy**: What are gliders?

**Lewis**: They're like airplanes, but without motors. They're like big kites, really.

**Tammy**: So why are the Wright brothers here at Kitty Hawk?

**Lewis**: Why don't you ask them?

**Tommy**: It looks as if the Wright brothers are having problems.

**Orville**: Nuts! Nuts! Nuts! The rudder is stuck again.

**Wilbur**: It's the sand, Orville. Why couldn't we do this back home in Ohio?

**Orville**: Who's flying this plane, you or me?

**Wilbur**: You are, Orville. But why do we have to do it in the sand?

**Orville**: Because if I crash, I want to crash on sand. It's softer.

**Wilbur**: You're right, Orville.

**Orville**: Who are these people?

**Tammy**: We're from the future.

**Lewis**: We came in our *When Machine.*

**Wilbur**: What's a *When Machine?*

**Tammy**: Lewis invented it. It's a machine that lets you go to any year and any place you want.

**Tommy**: Can we help?

**Orville**: Yes. You can help me get this rudder unstuck.

**Lewis**: Let's all try together.

**All**: One, two, three, pull!

**Wilbur**: It's free!

**Tammy**: Now the plane will fly. Right?

**Orville**: You know, maybe this isn't such a good idea after all.

**Tommy**: What's the matter?

**Wilbur**: I think Orville's still scared.

**Orville**: I'm not scared. I just don't know if it will fly.

**Lewis**: But you've been working on this for years.

**Wilbur**: We've tested gliders and kites.

**Orville**: We even built a wind tunnel to test the wings.

**Tammy**: A wind tunnel? What's that?

**Orville**: It's where you test the wings to see if they will lift you up or drag you down.

**Wilbur**: We call that lift and drag.

**Tommy**: Is that important?

**Orville**: It sure is. We need lift to get us off the ground.

**Wilbur**: The wings on our airplane are just wooden frames with cloth on them.

**Orville**: We can't flap them up and down.

**Wilbur**: No one has ever flown with an engine before, either.

**Tammy**: Why don't we go through the final checklist together?

**Lewis**: OK. Let's see. Are the wings strong and light?

**Orville**: They are very strong, and so light that one person can lift them.

**Tammy**: How good is your engine?

**Wilbur**: It's the best 1903 engine there is. We built it in our bicycle shop.

**Tommy**: How do you steer the plane?

**Orville**: I lie on the wing and move these ropes with my hands and feet.

**Wilbur**: Well, will it fly?

**Lewis**: I say yes. Tommy?

**Tommy**: I think it will fly. Tammy?

**Tammy**: Yes!

**Orville**: Our goal is to stay in the air for one minute.

**Wilbur**: What do you think, Orville? Ready to make history?

**Orville**: Let's go for it!

**Tommy**: What else can we do?

**Wilbur**: We need someone to turn the propeller.

**Tammy**: We'll all do it!

**Lewis**: It's turning.

**Orville**: Now, Wilbur, stand up ahead with the others. That way I'll know if I'm going straight.

**Wilbur**: OK. Here we go!

**Orville**: I'm picking up speed!

**Tammy**: It's starting to lift off the ground!

**Orville**: Wilbur, it's flying! It's flying!

**Wilbur**: Keep the wings straight!

**Tommy**: You're doing great, Orville!

**Lewis**: Be careful with the landing!

**Orville**: We did it! We flew for a whole minute!

**Tommy**: And this is just the beginning.

**Wilbur**: Soon we'll be able to fly from one town to another.

**Tammy**: Soon people will be flying all around the world.

**Orville**: Really?

**Tommy**: They'll fly in giant planes that carry more than 200 people.

**Tammy**: The planes will have jet engines and travel faster than sound.

**Lewis**: One day we'll even fly to the Moon and back.

**Wilbur**: To the Moon? How?

**Lewis**: Why don't you come visit us in the future? You can see for yourselves.

**Orville**: We'd like that. But right now we have a lot more work to do.

**Tammy**: OK. Well, good luck!

**Orville**: You, too!

**Wilbur**: Thanks for the help!

**Orville**: Where are you going to take your *When Machine* next?

**Lewis**: We don't know. But wherever it is, I'm going, too.

**All**: Good-bye!

**The End**

**READER'S THEATER**
**Multileveled Scripts**

# GLOSSARY

**airplane** (AIR-playn): a vehicle with wings and an engine that flies through the air

**engine** (EN-juhn): a machine that changes an energy source such as gasoline into movement

**gliders** (GLYE-durz): very light airplanes without engines that fly by floating and rising on air currents

**propeller** (pruh-PEL-ur): a set of rotating blades that provide force to move an airplane through air

**rudder** (RUHD-ur): a hinged wood or metal plate attached to the back of an airplane for steering

**wings** (WINGZ): large, flat structures on each side of an airplane that make it able to fly

# Under the Sea with Jacques Cousteau

## Summary

In this fantasy set deep beneath the ocean's surface, a group of sea creatures are discussing their own peculiar characteristics. When the arrival of Jacques Cousteau aboard his boat *Calypso* is announced by Dolphin, there is both confusion and excitement. Not all the creatures know about the famous ocean explorer. After they learn about him and the reason for his visit, the creatures speculate on whom he will choose to star in his TV show. Each creature attempts to impress Cousteau with its personality and feats. Cousteau reminds the group that they are all interesting and important.

# Under the Sea with Jacques Cousteau

## Objectives

### Literacy

**Students will:**

- Develop fluency and expression
- Understand characters' motives, actions, and feelings
- Relate what they know about marine life to their reading

### Science

**Students will:**

- Learn about marine life
- Understand some of the reasons why types of marine life are endangered

### Character Education

**Students will learn about:**

- **Respect**—deal peacefully with disagreements
- **Open-mindedness**—listen to new ideas

| Characters | Reading Levels |
|---|---|
| Starfish | F |
| Clam | F |
| Coral | G |
| Seaweed | G |
| Puffer Fish | H |
| Shark | H |
| Jacques Cousteau | I |
| Crab | I |
| Turtle | J |
| Dolphin | K |
| Octopus | L |
| Whale | M |

# Background Information

## Jacques Cousteau

Jacques Cousteau (1910–1997) was a French naval officer, marine explorer, author, and documentary filmmaker. His documentaries won forty Emmy nominations, and he hosted his own TV show, "Under the Sea." Cousteau also worked as an inventor to improve scuba gear, underwater photography, and diving safety—for example, by creating underwater cages for photographers. His films and philosophy educated people of all ages about ocean life and endangered ocean species. He worked well into his eighties, continually trying to build awareness about threatened areas on our planet.

## Endangered Marine Life

### Coral Reefs

Coral reefs provide homes for about a third of all fish species on Earth. They also play a major role in protecting coastlines from erosion. Coral reefs are made up of thousands of tiny animals called coral polyps. As these tiny animals die, new coral attach themselves to the skeletons of the dead animals.

Coral reefs are in danger for several reasons. Deforestation produces erosion that smothers the reef. Tourists and scuba divers often damage sensitive coral. Reefs are also affected by global warming and warm waters.

The World Wildlife Fund is currently working to ensure that ten percent of Earth's ocean area has protected status, a move that will benefit the coral.

### Sea Turtles

Although sea turtles have inhabited the planet for more than 100 million years, their future may be in danger. Many turtles get caught in shrimp trawler nets and drown. A device called a turtle excluder, which is a kind of hatch door that allows a turtle to escape before it drowns, is being used to protect the turtles. This is effective ninety-seven percent of the time.

Many sea turtles develop a disease that scientists believe may be linked to polluted waters. Sea turtles also eat plastic refuse, which can kill them.

Sea turtles lay their eggs on the shore. Poachers often take the eggs before they hatch. Those turtles that do hatch are often confused by city lights and go the wrong way, never making it to the sea.

# Staging and Performance Suggestions

- This script allows for a gradual introduction of characters onto the staging area. Begin with the characters of Puffer Fish, Crab, Clam, and Seaweed on stage. Direct the other characters to walk on and join the group as their parts dictate.

- Hang a blue sheet or blanket as the backdrop for the reading, or instruct students to paint an appropriate mural to be used as the backdrop. The mural can later be used as a place for students to hang their written and/or art work completed as part of the theme.

- Use small boxes as props to represent Cousteau's cameras.

# Literacy Extensions

## Research and Write

Ask students to choose an endangered animal they are interested in learning about. Tell them to research why it is in trouble and what is being done to protect it. When students finish their research, instruct them to create a poster that encourages people to protect the endangered animal.

## Sing about the Sea

Help students learn and sing the song "Calypso" by John Denver. Discuss why John Denver might have wanted to compose a tribute to Cousteau. Ask students to examine the words in the song and discuss how the words relate to Cousteau and his life's work.

# Content Connections

## Physical Science

Ocean water covers about three-quarters of Earth's surface. In fact, the oceans contain most of Earth's water—ninety-seven percent.

Ocean water contains many salts dissolved in the water. The most common salt is sodium chloride, which is the salt used to flavor food.

# Character Education Connection

- The sea creatures show friendship when they talk about each other. Write your name on a sheet of paper and trade with several classmates. On each person's paper, write one of his or her strengths. Then read your paper to find out what others think are your strengths.

- The sea creatures disagree peacefully. They stay calm and in control. With a partner, role-play a problem, such as friends both wanting to read the same book. How can you fix the problem peacefully?

- The sea creatures showed open-mindedness when they listened to each other. Why do we need to be open-minded? How do you show you are open to new ideas?

# Under the Sea
## with Jacques Cousteau

**CHARACTERS**

Puffer Fish

Crab

Clam

Seaweed

Coral

Octopus

Dolphin

Turtle

Whale

Shark

Starfish

Jacques Cousteau

**SETTING**

Under the sea, 1968

**Puffer Fish**: Good morning, Crab! What's up?

**Crab**: Oh, nothing exciting. I'm just looking for food down here. How about you, Puffer Fish?

**Puffer Fish**: Just swimming around.

**Clam**: Are you going to puff up? It's so amazing when you do that.

**Puffer Fish**: I hope I don't have to. I puff up only when I'm in danger, you know.

**Clam**: When I'm in danger, I clam up. Get it?

**Seaweed**: Very funny, Clam.

**Crab**: When I'm in danger, I scuttle away.

**Coral**: Scuttle? What does that mean?

**Crab**: It means I move sideways. You know, crabs are the only animals in the sea that can do that.

**Seaweed**: Really?

**Octopus**: I beg to differ with you, Crab. I may not have ten legs that bend in funny ways like yours do, but I can move sideways, too. I can move any way I want to. All I have to do is fill up with water and then shoot the water out. WHOOSH! There I go!

**Dolphin:** Hey, you guys! Listen up! I've got important news!

**Puffer Fish**: News? We haven't had any news in such a long time!

**Seaweed**: What is it, Dolphin?

**Coral**: Come closer so I can hear.

**Turtle**: Wait for me! Wait for me! I want to hear, too.

**Dolphin**: I was just at the surface with some of my dolphin friends. We were leaping and playing. We call that porpoising—even though we're not porpoises. We saw a big boat. It's right above us. It's the *Calypso*.

**Clam**: The what?

**Dolphin**: The *Calypso*. It's Jacques Cousteau's boat.

**Coral**: Jacques Cousteau? Who's that?

**Dolphin**: You've never heard of him?

**Seaweed**: Neither have I.

**Puffer Fish**: I hate to admit it, but I don't know who he is, either.

**Whale**: May I join your conversation? I was just swimming by and overheard you with my sonar. I can tell you who Jacques Cousteau is. He's the famous ocean explorer. He loves the sea. He has since he was a boy.

**Seaweed**: How do you know this, Whale?

**Whale**: I know whales that know whales that knew Jacques Cousteau when he was growing up in France.

**Dolphin**: He's also an inventor. He helped invent the scuba gear that divers use underwater. You've seen divers, haven't you?

**Coral**: I have.

**Seaweed**: Me, too.

**Clam**: Uh-oh. Here comes Shark.

**Shark**: Don't panic. I'm not here to eat anyone. I just happened to hear you talking. I know something else Jacques Cousteau invented: a special cage. It protects divers.

**Whale**: That's true. You see, Jacques Cousteau is also a photographer. He brings cameras underwater to take pictures. Sometimes he uses the cage.

**Turtle**: One night last year, I crawled onto a beach to lay my eggs. I heard some scientists talking about Jacques Cousteau. He has a new TV show. It's called "Under the Sea." It's about plants and animals like us.

**Clam**: He sounds amazing.

**Crab**: I'd like to meet him.

**Clam**: Me, too. But surely he wouldn't care about a little clam like me.

**Seaweed**: Or a little plant like me.

**Coral**: Or me. People who come here just want to break off parts of me.

**Puffer Fish**: I know, Coral. It's terrible. They don't realize that many plants and animals couldn't survive without you. Maybe Jacques Cousteau could help.

**Seaweed**: That would be great!

**Turtle**: Yes, but he's not coming to look at Coral. He's probably coming down to film me. Sea turtles are endangered, you know. And we're also fascinating. I'm more than 70 years old. Some sea turtles are even older.

**Puffer Fish**: Hey! You're not the only interesting one. What about me? I can swallow water and puff up to more than twice my size.

**Crab**: Puffer Fish has a point. He is very impressive when he does that. I've seen him scare away lots of creatures.

**Starfish**: But only one of us can be the star. It has to be me.

**Octopus**: And why is that?

**Starfish**: Because I'm a starfish.

**Octopus**: So? You may be a star, but do you have star power?

**Starfish**: I don't know. I never thought about that.

**Crab**: I think you do! You can move in any direction without turning. That's pretty cool.

**Starfish**: Thanks, Crab. Thanks for the support. You're pretty cool, too.

**Clam**: Yeah. Remember, you can scuttle. People would like to see that.

**Octopus**: I know you all want to be the star. But I'm sure Jacques Cousteau has come to film me. He'll want his TV viewers to see me up close. They can count my arms. They can see my suckers. I can disappear in a cloud of purple-black ink.

**Crab**: He's right. He sure has star power.

**Seaweed**: I guess so.

**Whale**: He's not the only one. Look how big I am. I weigh 200 tons! Plus, I'm a mammal. I breathe air, just like humans do. And my relatives have been around for 50 million years. We used to be dinosaurs!

**Crab**: I didn't know that.

**Shark**: Sharks were dinosaurs, too! We've been around for 100 million years. And I'm the best hunter. People want to see my sharp teeth up close.

**Dolphin**: I'm a mammal like Whale, but I hear a lot better. I can hear everything in the sea. I can dive 1,000 feet. And I can leap out of the water. Who else can do that?

**Clam**: Shhh! All of you. Look!

**Seaweed**: What is it?

**Turtle**: He's here!

**Coral**: Who?

**Turtle**: Jacques Cousteau!

**Shark**: And he's carrying his cameras!

**Dolphin**: Welcome, Mr. Cousteau!

**Crab**: We're so happy to see you.

**Octopus**: At least most of us are.

**Cousteau**: And I'm always happy to see my friends under the sea. But is everything OK? It sounded as if you were fighting just now.

**Puffer Fish**: We were fighting about who should be the star of your show.

**Cousteau**: The star of my TV show?

**Turtle**: I said it would probably be me. Right?

**Octopus**: Don't listen to him, Mr. Cousteau. I would make a much better star. I have star power.

**Whale**: People love to watch whales.

**Dolphin**: I saw your boat first. They wouldn't even know you were coming if it weren't for me.

**Crab**: I'm probably not interesting.

**Seaweed**: Me neither.

**Cousteau**: Please, everyone, stop your fighting. You're all interesting. You're all stars, as far as I'm concerned.

**Clam**: We are?

**Starfish**: Really? Even little me?

**Seaweed**: And me?

**Coral**: I'm a star like the others?

**Cousteau**: Each and every one of you is an important part of life under the sea. You all have incredible stories to tell. You're all stars. That's why I'm here. So let's get started.
Three... two... one... Action!

**The End**

# GLOSSARY

**camera** (KAM-er-uh): a device used to take photographs or motion pictures

**divers** (DYE-vurz): people who work or explore underwater with special equipment

**endangered** (en-DAYN-jerd): put in danger

**explorer** (ik-SPLOHR-er): a person who travels through an unfamiliar place for the purpose of discovery

**scuba gear** (SKOO-buh GEAR): equipment used for breathing underwater [*self-contained underwater breathing apparatus*]

**sonar** (SOH-nar): a system that uses sound waves to locate underwater objects [*sound navigation and ranging*]

# Reader's Theater Rubric

| Rating Scale | **Phrasing and Fluency** |
|:---:|:---|
| 1 | Reads word by word. Does not attend to author's syntax or sentence structures. Has limited sense of phrase boundaries. |
| 2 | Reads slowly and in a choppy manner, usually in two-word phrases. Some attention is given to author's syntax and sentence structures. |
| 3 | Reads in phrases of three to four words. Appropriate syntax is used. |
| 4 | Reads in longer, more meaningful phrases. Regularly uses pitch, stress, and author's syntax to reflect comprehension. |

| | **Intonation** |
|:---:|:---|
| 1 | Reads in a monotone and does not attend to punctuation. |
| 2 | Reads with some intonation and some attention to punctuation. Reads in a monotone at times. |
| 3 | Reads by adjusting intonation appropriately. Consistently attends to punctuation. |
| 4 | Reads with intonation that reflects feeling, anticipation, tension, character development, and mood. |

| | **Listening** |
|:---:|:---|
| 1 | Does not listen attentively and cannot provide relevant suggestions to improve readings of others. Is disruptive. |
| 2 | Listens most of the time but has difficulty commenting on the readings of others. |
| 3 | Listens to the readings of others without interruption. Makes some suggestions for ways to improve readings. Needs help clarifying own ideas and ideas of others. |
| 4 | Listens to the readings of others without interruption. Comments positively on the readings and makes appropriate suggestions for improvement. Seeks clarification when something is not understood. Clarifies own comments when not understood by others, using such phrasing as "what I meant was…" |

| | **Pace** |
|:---:|:---|
| 1 | Slow and laborious reading. |
| 2 | Reading is either moderately slow or inappropriately fast. |
| 3 | Unbalanced combination of slow and fast reading. |
| 4 | Reading is consistently natural, conversational, and appropriate (resembling natural oral language). |

| Rating Scale | **Accuracy** |
|:---:|:---|
| 1 | Multiple attempts at decoding words without success. Word reading accuracy is inadequate/poor, below 85%. |
| 2 | Attempts to self-correct errors, usually unsuccessful. Word reading accuracy is marginal, between 86%–90%. |
| 3 | Attempts to self-correct errors are successful. Word reading accuracy is good, between 91%–95%. |
| 4 | Most words are read correctly on initial attempt. Minimal self-corrections, all successful. Word reading accuracy is excellent, 96% and above. |

## Characterization

| | |
|:---:|:---|
| 1 | Has difficulty understanding the characters and cannot portray them accurately. |
| 2 | Can characterize accurately those characters presented in a straightforward way but has difficulty making inferences, even with teacher guidance. |
| 3 | Can characterize accurately those characters presented in a straightforward way. With teacher guidance, can understand more subtle characteristics and make inferences about characters in a given situation. |
| 4 | Makes accurate inferences and interpretations about characters, using appropriate voice, tone, expression, and body language. |

## Behavior

| | |
|:---:|:---|
| 1 | Cannot work independently when others are rehearsing or working with the teacher. When in a group situation, needs continual reminders of rehearsal and performance expectations. Has difficulty working with other students: doesn't take turns, speaks at inappropriate times, doesn't listen, is disruptive and distracting. |
| 2 | Tries to work independently, but is occasionally disruptive. Sometimes forgets rehearsal and performance expectations. Has some difficulty working with others. |
| 3 | Usually works quietly and responsibly when others are rehearsing. Understands expectations and follows through most of the time. Usually works well with others. |
| 4 | Works quietly and responsibly on independent activities when others are rehearsing or working with the teacher. Understands rehearsal and performance expectations and acts on them. Works well with others. |